# Almost Enough



Zaubia Rahman

Qurate
quratebooks.com

**ALMOST ENOUGH**

Zaubia Rahman



Published in 2025

© Published by

**Qurate Books Pvt. Ltd.**

Goa 403523, India

www.quratebooks.com

Tel: 1800-210-6527, Email: info@quratebooks.com



**ISBN:** 978-93-58981-91-9

# Phase 1

In shadows deep where whispers weave,
Rehal stood, a heart to grieve.
"Zoa," he called, his voice a plea,
"Why do you dance just out of reach?"

She turned, a flash of sapphire eyes,
"Rehal, you know it's not a lie.
I feel your weight, your longing gaze,
But love's a fire, I cannot blaze."

With clenched fists, he took a step,
“Why can’t you see? My heart’s adept!
It beats for you, it craves your touch,
Yet you pull back, it hurts so much.”

Zoa sighed, a fragile sound,
“Your heart’s a storm, it spins around.
But I am fragile, I’m not so bold,
Love feels like chains, too heavy, too cold.”

"Chains?" he echoed, voice like thunder,
"Is that how you see my love? I wonder.
I want to keep you, safe and near,
Not lock you up, but hold you dear."

Her laughter danced, a bitter note,
"Safe? Or possess? You seem to gloat.
You think I'm weak, a flower in hand,
But I'm a soul, not made to command."

“Then why,” he growled, “do you run away?
You tease the sun, then hide in grey.
I’m not your enemy; don’t you see?
I’m what you need; I’m meant to be!”

Zoa’s breath hitched, a flicker of doubt,
“Do you love me, or just the clout?
I’m not a trophy, a prize to claim,
I’m tired of playing your twisted game.”

"Twisted? No," he snapped with a frown,
"I'm just a boy who's lost in this town.
You're a light, a spark in my darkened night,
Without you, Zoa, nothing feels right."

She took a step back, her heart in a vise,
"Rehal, your love feels like a disguise.
I can't breathe when you're so near,
Your grasp is tight; it chokes my fear."

"Fear?" he echoed, eyes wide with rage,
"Or is it freedom? Turn the page!
I'll give you everything, just take my hand,
Together, we can make our own stand."

Zoa shook her head, tears in her eyes,
"Your love feels like a prison, not the skies.
You think you're saving, but you're holding me down,
With every embrace, I start to drown."

"Drown?" he scoffed, "I'm your lifeline!
Without me, Zoa, you'll never shine.
You're lost in the dark; I'm the one who fights,
I'll fill the space, I'll light the nights."

"Fill the space?" she spat, voice taut,
"You fill the air with the battles you've fought.
But love isn't war; it's not a decree,
It's a dance, Rehal, it's meant to be free."

His face turned stormy, a cloud of despair,
"Then how do I reach you? It feels so unfair!
I'm desperate, Zoa; I'm caught in this game,
Your heart's a riddle that drives me insane."

"Desperate?" she whispered, a sharp little knife,
"Your love's a tempest, it cuts like a strife.
I want to be loved, not held under glass,
Not just a dream that you want to amass."

With a roar, he stormed, “Then what do you need?
A different boy? Someone to concede?
I’m all that I am, and I’m all that you’ve got,
If you push me away, I’ll wither and rot.”

Zoa’s voice trembled, “No one’s asking for more,
But the love that you give feels like a war.
I want to feel cherished, not bound by your chains,
I want to be wanted, not filled with your pains.”

"Pain?" he cried, "Is that what I bring?
I thought I was offering you everything.
What if I change? What if I bend?
I can be gentle, I can pretend."

"Pretend?" she scoffed, "That's not what I seek,
I need a connection, not someone weak.
You're strong in your ways, but lost in your mind,
You can't force a heart; it's cruel and unkind."

"Then teach me," he begged, eyes wide with need,
"Show me the way; I'll follow your lead.
I'll learn how to love, how to let you be free,
Just promise me, Zoa, you won't abandon me."

She paused, her breath caught in the air,
Could love be a choice? Could they ever be fair?
"Rehal," she murmured, "it's more than just this,
It's trust, it's a bond, it's the sweet taste of bliss."

"I'll trust you," he vowed, "if you trust me too.
I'll fight for your heart; I'll always be true.
I'll fill the space that you can't reach,
Just promise me, Zoa, you'll never breach."

"Breaching feels like breaking," she said with a sigh,
"I'm scared of the edge; I'm scared of the high.
But if there's a chance, if there's a way,
I'll meet you halfway; I'll learn how to stay."

Rehal's heart soared, a flicker of hope,
"Then let's take this journey, let's learn how to cope.
I'll be the anchor, you'll be the sail,
Together we'll weather this ominous gale."

With hands interlocked, they faced the abyss,
A dance of two souls, a fragile kiss.
"Let's fill the space," murmured Zoa, unsure,
"Together, we'll find what we're longing for."

In the dark, they wandered, side by side,
Learning to love, learning to bide.
Each laugh a spark, each tear a release,
As they navigated the chaos, they found their peace.

Though shadows lingered, and doubt still loomed,
Their hearts intertwined; their love had bloomed.
“Rehal,” she whispered, “I’ll take the risk,
In this dance of ours, I’ll learn how to whisk.”

"Zoa," he breathed, "you fill my heart,
In this space we share, we'll never part.
I'll hold you close, I'll let you be free,
Together, we'll fill what's meant to be."

And so they journeyed, through thick and through thin,
A dance of love, where both could begin.
In the space they filled, they learned to reach,
For love is a lesson, it's always a teach.

Through laughter and pain, through joy and despair,
They filled the void with the love they would share.
In shadows deep, where whispers weave,
Zoa and Rehal learned how to believe.

# Filling a space I can’t reach

## Phase 2

In a town where shadows dance and cling,
Rehal walked with a heart that could sting.
His gaze, a storm, yearning to breach,
A longing so deep, it felt out of reach.

“Zoa,” he whispered, beneath the pale moon,
“Your laughter’s a melody, a haunting tune.”
But she turned, a smile like a flickering flame,
“Rehal, you know, love’s not a game.”

Yet he pressed, with eyes ablaze,
“Don’t you feel it? This fiery gaze?”
“Rehal,” she sighed, a hint of despair,
“There’s a space in my heart that’s empty and bare.”

“Then let me fill it,” he said with a plea,
“Every moment I’m lost in what we could be.”
But the more he reached, the more she withdrew,
A dance of desire, a heart breaking through.

"Can't you see?" she cried, a tremor in voice,
"I'm trapped in a silence, with no other choice."
He clenched his fists, the darkness unfurled,
"Zoa, you're the sun; you're my whole world."

"Rehal, you smother," she whispered, afraid,
"This love that you offer, it feels like a blade."
But he stepped closer, a shadow in night,
"Without you, my darling, I'm losing the fight."

"Your love is a prison, I can't escape,"
"Yet still, I am drawn, like a moth to a shape."
"Zoa, don't run; let me hold you tight,
I'll fill every corner, I'll banish the night."

With a sigh, she murmured, "It's not that I fear,
It's the weight of your wanting that's drawing me near."
Yet the distance between them was thicker than fog,
A silence so heavy, it felt like a log.

"Why can't you see?" he echoed her pain,
"Every moment without you drives me insane."
"Rehal," she breathed, "this isn't a game,
You can't own my heart; you can't stake your claim."

His voice grew a growl, dark and intense,
"Zoa, I'm desperate; this doesn't make sense."
With each passing second, the tension would swell,
A love that was sweet, now tangled in hell.

"Can't you feel it?" he asked, eyes ablaze,
"This pull, this hunger, this fevered craze?"
"I feel it," she whispered, her breath caught in flight,
"But it's a storm, Rehal, it's not black and white."

"Then let's color it in," he offered with rage,
"I'll break down the walls, I'll write every page."
But she shook her head, a tear in her eye,
"Love isn't a chapter; it can't be a lie."

"Zoa, you're leaving, don't walk out that door,"
"Can't you hear my heart? It's begging for more!"
"Rehal," she sighed, "I'm not the one you seek,
Your love is a fortress, yet mine feels so weak."

"I'll build you a castle," he promised, so sure,
"Just let me inside; let me be your cure."
But she stepped back, the distance a chasm,
"It's not that simple; it's not some grand spasm."

"Then tell me, my love, what must I become?"
"Do I shed all my layers, become numb?"
"No," she replied, her voice soft yet firm,
"Love should nurture, not twist and not squirm."

"Zoa, just give me a chance to explain,
I'm not just a boy; I'm a heart filled with pain."
"Pain isn't love, Rehal; it's a mirror of fear,
And love should uplift, not draw us near tears."

"Then what do you want?" he barked, a wild beast,
"Do you want me to fade, to become the least?"
"I want you to listen, to see what's inside,
To understand that love isn't something to bide."

"Then why do I feel this possessiveness grow?"
"Because you're afraid of what you don't know."
"Zoa," he whispered, "don't walk away,
You're the only light that can brighten my day."

She turned, hesitating, a moment's reprieve,
"Rehal, it's not easy; I can't just believe."
"Then let me show you," he begged, reaching out,
"Love's a tempest, but it's not filled with doubt."

With a sigh, she spoke, her heart laid so bare,
"Love's not a conquest; it's not a snare."
"But I need you," he cried, desperation his song,
"Without you, my world feels endlessly wrong."

"Rehal," she murmured, "this darkness you wear,
It's heavy and burdensome; it's too much to bear."
"I'm trying," he answered, his voice filled with ache,
"To pull you in closer, to keep you awake."

"But love should be light," she countered with grace,
"Not a shadow that lingers, not a perilous chase."
"I'll change," he promised, his heart on the line,
"Just give me a chance; give love the right sign."

"Then start with yourself," she urged, calm and wise,
"Unravel the storm that curls in your eyes."
He closed them tightly, felt the weight of her truth,
"Zoa, for you, I'll fight through my youth."

"Then fight with your heart, not with possession,"
"Love isn't a war; it's a sweet progression."
"Stay with me," he pleaded, "let's find our way,
Together we'll conquer the night and the day."

"Together," she echoed, a glimmer of hope,
"But it starts with respect, a chance to elope."
"So take my hand, Zoa; let's step into light,
I'll fill every space, and we'll both take flight."

With cautious steps forward, they met in the dark,
A flicker of trust ignited a spark.
"I'll teach you to love," he promised, sincere,
"And together, my darling, we'll conquer the fear."

“Then let’s take this journey, one step at a time,
We’ll learn how to dance, we’ll learn how to rhyme.”
Rehal nodded, a smile breaking free,
“Together, my love, it’s just you and me.”

And so, in the shadows, they carved out their tale,
A love that would flourish, a ship set to sail.
No longer a battle, no longer confined,
Just two souls entwined, in the depths of their mind.

"Zoa," he whispered, the moon in their view,
"I'll cherish your heart, every moment with you."
"Rehal," she smiled, a warmth in her chest,
"I'll fill the spaces, together we'll rest."

In that quiet embrace, they found their own peace,
A love born from struggle, a sweet, tender lease.
With each step they took, they filled up the space,
No longer alone; they'd both found their place.

# Mine Always Mine

## Phase 3

In a world spun from silver and dreams,
Where the moonlight dances and the starlight beams,
There lived a girl, wild as the wind,
With eyes like the ocean, where secrets rescind.
Her name was Zoa, a spirit untamed,
In the garden of love, she sought to be claimed.

Rehal, a prince with a heart like the dawn,
Wandered through shadows, in search of a song,
With laughter like music, and warmth in his gaze,
He crossed through the mist and the shimmering haze.
In a realm where the flowers grew bright and divine,
Zoa whispered softly, “You’re mine, always mine.”

Their story began in a forest of dreams,
Where petals of light danced in shimmering streams.
With a heart full of wonder, Zoa reached out,
Entwining their destinies, erasing all doubt.
But the thread of possession wove in her heart,
As love turned to longing, and longing to art.

"Rehal," she breathed, in a breathless delight,
"In a world of shadows, you're my guiding light.
With you, I am fearless, my spirit takes flight,
In the depths of your eyes, I find infinite night."
Yet beneath her sweet words, a tempest did churn,
A hunger for more, a fierce need to yearn.

The stars bore witness to each fleeting glance,
As breezes whispered secrets, laced with romance.
But Zoa, enthralled, in her passion entwined,
Felt a fierce claim, the threads of love lined.
“Forever, dear Rehal, I promise to bind,
You’re not just my dream, you’re mine, always mine.”

With laughter and sunlight, their days intertwined,
They danced through the meadows, their spirits aligned.
Yet in the shadows, a whisper took flight,
A warning unspoken, veiled deep in the night.
For in loving too fiercely, the boundaries would blur,
And love, when possessive, can easily stir.

"Zoa," he chimed, "love should never be chains,
Let it be a river that joyfully gains.
I treasure each moment, but let's not confine,
For together, our hearts can forever entwine."
But Zoa, in passion, felt the stakes rise,
Her fingers entwined like the webs of the skies.

One evening, as twilight settled like breath,
A shadow crept forth—was it love, or was it death?
In the heart of the grove, where their secrets were laid,
A sorceress lingered, with intentions displayed.
"You bind him too close, sweet Zoa," she sang,
"Love should be gentle, not a sharp pang."

“Release him,” she warned, her voice low and clear,
“Or lose him forever, to shadows and fear.”
But Zoa, with fierceness, replied with a sigh,
“No enchantment can sever the bond held so high.
I’ll keep him, my treasure, through realms dark and bright,
For love is possession, my heart’s pure delight.”

Yet as the moon rose, a chill swept the land,
A crack in the magic, a slip from her hand.
Rehal grew distant, confusion his crown,
As Zoa held tighter, her world crumbling down.
Her love turned to shadows, a snare of despair,
Each whisper of longing now echoed in air.

"Zoa," he murmured, lost in the storm,
"I need you beside me, but not in this form.
Love's not a prison; it's wings that we wear,
In the vastness of freedom, love's tender care."
But Zoa, in panic, her heart turned to stone,
Fell deeper in madness, in a world of her own.

Days turned to weeks as a rift split the sky,
Despair like a fog, wrapping hearts in a lie.
Rehal, through the darkness, sought love's gentle light,
In dreams filled with whispers that echoed the night.
"Zoa, my darling, please hear my plea,
Your heart does not flourish when you're holding tightly."

Finally, when twilight embraced the deep sea,
Zoa stood alone, lost in fantasy,
Amongst the wild blossoms, under stars that did shine,
She grasped at the whisper, "You're mine, always mine."
But on the cool breeze, a memory stayed,
Of laughter and love that could not be frayed.

In the heart of her longing, the truth would unfold,
Love isn't possession; it's more precious than gold.
It swells like the ocean, wide and unconfined,
Transforming all boundaries, uniting the blind.
With a breath of the night and a tear in her eye,
She released all her fears, her heart to the sky.

“Rehal,” she called, a melody sweet,
“Come back to me, love, let our hearts meet.
No longer a shackle, but a bond that will shine,
You’re treasured and cherished; you’re always mine.”
And then like the dawn chasing shadows away,
Rehal appeared, with warmth of the day.

Their eyes locked in magic, the air thick with love,
A symphony whispered by stars up above.
“Zoa,” he breathed, with a heart wild and free,
“You’re the sun in my sky; you’re all parts of me.
Love can’t be owned, it’s a dance, it’s a fire,
Together we blossom, our spirits conspire.”

In a swirl of affection, they both understood,
Through lessons of heartache, they emerged as they stood.
With each gentle promise, with every entwined,
They embraced the pure essence that love had enshrined.
“No more do I claim you, nor you claim me too,
But in this sweet freedom, our love will renew.”

As the light of the moon painted silvered trails,
Their laughter echoed through enchanted gales.
Zoa, now radiant, felt his love unwind,
A tapestry woven, their lives intertwined.
“Mine,” she whispered, with her heart intertwined,
“Always yours, Rehal, our souls aligned.”

Lost in the magic, they danced ‘neath the stars,
With love as their compass, overcoming the scars.
In a world full of promise, both gentle and kind,
They flourished like flowers, forever entwined.
And in every heartbeat, in every sweet chime,
The truth of their love was, “Yours, always mine.”

Through kingdoms of dreams, their spirits took flight,
Zoa and Rehal, two souls ignited bright.
In the depths of forever, their hearts would align,
Embracing the wonder, “You’re mine, always mine.”